Devon's History

Robert Hesketh

Bossiney Books

Torquay Harbour about 1835, when coal was still delivered by sea
The photograph on the previous page is of Totnes Castle

Some other Bossiney titles about Devon's history

An absurdly short history of Exeter
Ancient Dartmoor
Cob and thatch
Devon place names
Devon smugglers
Devon's railways
Medieval Dartmoor
Sir Francis Drake – Devon's flawed hero
Torbay – the hidden history

This reprint 2012
First published 2009 by
Bossiney Books Ltd, 33 Queens Drive, Ilkley, LS29 9QW
www.bossineybooks.com
© 2009 Robert Hesketh   All rights reserved
ISBN 978-1-906474-14-0

Acknowledgements
All photographs are by the author or from the publishers' own collection,
except the following which are reproduced by kind permission:
page 37 the Beaford Archive; page 42 Chris Webber.

Printed in Great Britain by R Booth Ltd, Penryn, Cornwall

Introduction

Enjoying an isolated position far removed from the powerful influences of London, Devon developed in its own way. Even today it retains that distinctiveness, in its landscape, its own breeds of cattle, sheep and ponies, its characteristic dialect and its food and drink.

However, with superb natural anchorages along two coastlines, and several sheltered estuaries large enough to house a fleet, Devon has always been open to the wider world. Its ports have been crucial to the county's development. Dartmouth and later Plymouth guarded the Western Approaches, protecting the country from invasion and blockade. Devon has always been in the front line of naval warfare – most famously in combating the Spanish Armada of 1588. The county's role in the First and (especially) the Second World Wars was equally vital.

Devon thrived on overseas trade, fishing, sailing and shipbuilding, as well as exploration and colonisation of the New World. During Elizabeth I's reign a generation of Devon seamen, including Drake, Hawkins, Raleigh, Gilbert, Davis, Burroughs, Grenville and Oxenham, won lasting and international renown. As A L Rowse (a Cornishman!) wrote: 'The contribution of Devon men to the genius and achievement of the country has been prodigious.'

On a less swashbuckling note, Devon developed as England's leading seaside holiday county from the late 18th century. Its beautiful land and seascapes and (sometimes) mild climate have made it a magnet for those who seek a better world without leaving England.

There is a lot more to Devon than seaside. Between the coasts, some 70 miles (110 km) apart, is a huge hinterland of 1.66 million acres (672,000 hectares). As England's third largest county, it has a remarkable variety of topography, geology and climate; and thus of farming and settlement. In the fertile South Hams, Exe Valley and East Devon, arable and dairy farming prospered. Settlement is generally dense and villages large. By contrast, the poorly drained uplands of North and Mid-Devon's 'culm measures' contain isolated farms and small hamlets. The climate is wet and windy. Rough grazing and stock rearing predominate.

A wet climate favoured sheep rearing. Devon wool made cloth the county's chief industry and source of wealth for centuries, while its many rivers drove tucking (fulling) mills. Many of its inland towns and ports developed as cloth making or selling centres.

Stock rearing and dairy farming led to Devon's early enclosure and its patchwork of small fields. These had replaced most medieval open fields centuries before large scale enclosure up-country. Separated by high, stock-proof hedgebanks, built and steeped in a distinctively Devonian way, some follow prehistoric field boundaries. Narrow lanes (Devon has the highest road mileage of any shire county) wind between them, connecting scattered villages and farmsteads. The rich history of this distinctive landscape became the special study of the county's leading historian, W G Hoskins.

Much of Dartmoor and Exmoor, however, is unenclosed. Here, amid the highest, most rugged and thinly populated terrain in southern England, the average rainfall is up to three times the norm for sheltered Torbay or the lower Exe Valley. The high moors remain places apart with their own traditions, notably in building. Dartmoor's granite buildings include a rich prehistoric landscape of houses, monuments and field boundaries.

Elsewhere in Devon, the underlying rocks have determined local building materials. These range from the limestones of Plymouth and Torbay to the beautiful Beer stone of East Devon. However, great swathes of the county, especially in Mid- and North Devon, have no good building stones and earth walling in the West Country cob tradition predominates.

Geology has also given Devon hard rock mining. Tin and copper, along with a range of other valuable metals, were mined on Dartmoor and in North Devon. The county also yields ball and china clays in abundance. Indeed, the Bovey Basin has the world's largest reserves of ball clay.

1 Prehistoric Devon

Archaeology has revealed a fascinating and complex picture of prehistoric Devon. This is being enlarged and reassessed all the time, aided by technology, including aerial photography, carbon dating, geophysical survey, pollen analysis and computer imaging.

Kent's Cavern in Torquay is the best place to start the story of prehistoric Devon. These limestone caves are the richest Palaeolithic (Old Stone Age) site in the county, arguably in England, and also the oldest recognizable human dwelling in Britain. Oldest among the many finds at Kent's Cavern, including axes, saws, awls and scrapers, are five flint hand axes, approximately 450,000 years old, when our primitive ancestors *Homo erectus* walked the land.

The more advanced Neanderthals left tangible evidence of their lives too, principally flint implements, whilst the earliest evidence of modern man, *Homo sapiens*, is a jaw bone, dated 37-40,000 years old.

The Axe Valley, notably the gravel workings near Broom, has also yielded Palaeolithic finds in a primary (original) context – though there, as in Kent's Cavern, many were probably washed in by rain or river action. Over 1800 finds, including chert hand-axes, make up the single largest haul of Palaeolithic artefacts in the West Country, dated to approximately 280,000 years ago. Other Palaeolithic finds have been made in the Exe,

The Hurston double stone row. Dartmoor has 76 known stone rows, often with round cairns or long stones ('menhirs'), as well as 18 stone circles. The rows vary from a few metres in length to over three kilometres

Otter and Teign valleys, Windmill Hill, Brixham, and caves at Torbryan and Plymouth.

The Mesolithic (Middle Stone Age), c7500BC-3500BC, has produced more plentiful and widely distributed finds in Devon, particularly on Dartmoor and in river valleys. Traditionally, the Mesolithic was seen as the transitional period after the last Ice Age between the purely hunting and gathering nomadic life of the Palaeolithic and the adoption of a settled existence based on farming in the Neolithic (New Stone Age).

Although archaeologists generally agree that domestic animals were important in Neolithic Devon (c4500-2200BC) – and there is abundant evidence from bones to show they were – many now question the importance of agriculture. Nomadic hunting life and a meat-based diet did not suddenly cease. It is more probable that during the Neolithic period people on the northern fringes of European agriculture gradually adopted farming, as and when it suited local conditions, using a crude 'slash and burn' technique to clear woodland. On Dartmoor, this resulted in the destruction of much tree cover and the creation of extensive peat bogs.

Evidence from the Neolithic is much greater than for the far longer earlier periods. Neolithic finds, mainly stone tools such as axes and arrow heads, are scattered through Devon. Pottery, a Neolithic development which also survives well, has been found in quantity too.

Hembury in East Devon, where crops were grown at the early Neolithic date of 4200BC, is among several Neolithic causewayed enclosures. Another interesting site consists of the foundations of a rectangular house on top of Haldon. On this very exposed and windswept position the views are magnificent, but the soil is not. This is not the sort of place where Neolithic domestic settlements are normally found. It is more likely to have been a mainly ceremonial site built as a focal point and visible for a great distance around.

Four Neolithic 'shilstones' – communal chambered graves built of large stone slabs with heavy capstones, formerly known as 'cromlechs' – survive in Devon. Spinsters' Rock near Drewsteignton is the best example. Four more settlement sites retain the name Shilstone ('shelf stone'), so these are probably 'lost' sites. Spinsters' Rock is but one part of Dartmoor's very rich prehistoric heritage. Unfortunately, it is difficult to date 'hut circles', which are the foundations of prehistoric round houses or outbuildings. Within northern Europe this house design is unique to Britain and Ireland. Some 5000 are estimated to survive on Dartmoor, varying in diameter from 1.5 m to a massive 11 m. Some stand alone, others in villages of 60 or more. Experimental reconstructions of round houses, using the materials available to prehistoric peoples, prove that they were remarkably robust, weatherproof and spacious.

Although Dartmoor's ceremonial sites do not contain such large standing stones as the most famous sites like Avebury and Stonehenge in Wiltshire, there are many of them and they are very impressive in the wild moorland landscape.

Some of Dartmoor's round houses and ceremonial sites may be Neolithic, but the majority probably belong to the succeeding Bronze Age, c 2200 BC-700 BC. Dartmoor also possesses over 400 km of Early Bronze Age 'reaves', field boundary banks of stone and earth, forming the best preserved and most complete prehistoric field system in Britain, perhaps in Europe. Used for grazing, these fields may also have supported some crops, as suggested by the presence of 'lynchets', low earth banks.

The largest of these reave systems covers 20 km² and includes 25 separate round houses. Usually reaves are laid out in dead straight lines, accurate to within one degree – a remarkable achievement of both surveying and social organisation, but we always tend to underestimate our prehistoric ancestors! Some reaves still form the boundaries of Dartmoor farms.

The harsh climate of high Dartmoor and Exmoor has helped preserve prehistoric monuments – in particular it has protected them from plough damage – and made them the richest areas for discovered prehistoric sites in Devon. This has led many people to assume that, whilst Dartmoor and Exmoor were densely settled, lowland Devon was left largely uninhabited and thickly forested. Recent evidence from aerial photographs and geophysical research, combined with intensive field work, has shown that settlement in Devon was more widespread than previously thought. The complex of late Neolithic/Early Bronze Age sites around Bow and North Tawton are a case in point.

Whether tin and copper, the constituents of bronze, were mined or streamed on Dartmoor during the Bronze Age is an intriguing question. Unfortunately, later working on Dartmoor, especially medieval tin streaming along the river banks, was so prolonged and intense, leaving so much debris, that it destroyed possible evidence of earlier working.

An ancient shipwreck at the mouth of the river Erme in South Devon makes the question of where the bronze used in Devon came from – or where it was going to – even more tantalising. The wreck, possibly the oldest ever discovered in Britain, included 42 ingots of almost pure tin, each weighing between 0.5 and 13kg and all formed in earthen moulds. The ingots were dated to between 1000 BC (Late Bronze Age) and AD 400 (towards the end of the Roman period). We may speculate on their source and destination, but the wreck strongly suggests overseas trade. Cornish metals were known in the ancient world from at least the 4th century BC. British metals were a prime motive for the Roman conquest.

Important Early Bronze Age (2500 BC-1600 BC) finds at Plymstock, including axes, tools, daggers and a single spearhead, have led to that period being called the Plymstock Phase. By the same token, the Middle Bronze Age (1600 BC-1200 BC) is referred to locally as the Chagford or Taunton phase, whilst the late Bronze Age (1200 BC-900 BC) is called the Worth or Dainton phase. The last period of the Bronze Age (900 BC-600 BC) is the Mount Batten, after the hill east of Plymouth.

Settlements called rounds, basically fortified farmsteads with single ramparts typical of the Iron Age (c 600 BC-AD 43), are common in Cornwall and some have been found in Devon recently. However, the Iron Age in Devon is characterised by its hill forts. There are approximately a hundred. Some, like Embury near Hartland and Bolt near Salcombe, are cliff castles; others such as Hembury and Woodbury in East Devon are large tribal hill forts with ditches and ramparts. Most of this type are east of the Exe and concentrated near the Dorset boundary. Some may have belonged to the people of Dorset (*Durotriges*) rather than the *Dumnonii* of what later became Devon and Cornwall. Many have names ending in 'bury': Woodbury, Hembury, Blackbury, Musbury, Sidbury and Membury.

Woodbury Castle is a classic Iron Age hill fort, built between 500 and 300 BC in a splendid defensive position overlooking the East Devon Commons, the Exe and the coast. Its ramparts, imposing even in ruin, were once much higher and topped with timber palisades. They sheltered a permanent settlement of wooden houses, probably centred on the home of a local chief. In times of strife it was a place of refuge.

Exploiting a natural defensive site on a greensand spur, Hembury Fort (5km north-west of Honiton) is also a great viewpoint. Like Woodbury, it remains impressive, with high ramparts and deep ditches. These belong principally to the Iron Age, but Hembury is one of many sites successively occupied in different historical periods.

Archaeologists have radio-carbon-dated a Neolithic palisade and ditch at Hembury to 3300 BC-3100 BC. They also discovered pottery and a cache

Blackdown Rings, near Loddiswell in the South Hams. This well preserved Iron Age fort was re-occupied by the Norman conquerors, who used its ditches as a bailey and built a motte within

of slingstones near the gateways, as well as evidence that the Romans used the fort in the early stages of their western campaign (before AD 50).

2 Romano-British Devon

Archaeologists have also revised their interpretations of Devon's Roman period in the light of recent discoveries. *Dumnonia*, the area which later became Devon and Cornwall, was less Romanised than the south-east of England. However, the influence of Rome, whilst often building on what was already here such as the hillfort at Hembury, was greater than previously known. Recent research, including aerial photography, has shown the Romans had a substantial military presence in Devon well beyond their central base at Exeter. This comprised ten known forts, one possible fort, two temporary camps, two fortlets each big enough for a small detachment, three possible fortlets and two possible ports, in addition to the known port of Topsham.

Countisbury's Roman signal station at Old Barrow on the North Devon coast is a good example. Built with customary Roman thoroughness in the 1st century AD, it is a square enclosure with rounded angles, enclosed by a triple vallum and ditch. In conjunction with their other North Devon clifftop fortlet and signal station at Martinhoe, Old Barrow enabled soldiers to keep a watch on shipping, especially any seaborne attacks the warlike *Silures* of South Wales might attempt.

Some of the best preserved Roman sites outside Exeter, the chief settlement of the Romano-British period, are along the Dorset border – at Membury, Holcombe and Seaton. They include mosaic floors and baths, both Roman introductions. Holcombe also yielded a beautifully decorated Iron Age mirror, from a pit beneath the Romano-British villa, showing that this site, like many others, had been occupied before.

More recent excavations have revealed a variety of buildings in a complex at Topsham, plus a group of simple stone buildings at Otterton. Overall,

Roman material from findspots, excavations and coin hoards indicates extensive use of the countryside and thus a sizeable Devon population.

With the Romans, Devon's history enters the realm of written sources. These sources are neither flattering nor extensive. The only direct reference to the *Dumnonii* is very brief: Ptolemy in his *Geography* mentioned *Isca* (Exeter), *Tamaris* (Plymouth) and *Nemetostatio* (North Tawton), plus the rivers *Isca* (Exe) and *Tamarus* (Tamar).

Tacitus, the noted Roman historian, makes plain in his *Agricola* the main motive of conquest: 'Britain yields gold, silver and other metals, to make it worth conquering.' Neither British culture nor the British climate had any appeal: 'We are dealing with barbarians... The climate is objectionable, with its frequent rains and mists, but there is no extreme cold.'

Although Tacitus admired the hardihood and barbaric courage of the British tribes, he saw their lack of organisation – both military and political – as a fatal weakness. 'Nothing has helped us more in war with their strongest nations than their inability to co-operate. It is but seldom that two or three states unite to repel a common danger.'

The Roman conquest of *Britannia*, then a patchwork of tribal areas rather than a nation, began with the invasion of Kent in AD 43. Emperor Claudius' troops established military control in the south-east. His general, Vespasian, then led the Second Legion in a powerful drive south-west into the territory of the *Durotriges* (Dorset and part of Somerset), taking many towns and fortresses on the way.

The concentration of hillforts in East Devon on the border between *Dumnonia* and the *Durotriges'* territory suggests a hostile or at least a tense relationship between these neighbours. The astute Vespasian (later Emperor Vespasian) would no doubt have been quick to exploit any differences between the two tribes on the divide-and-rule principle.

Archaeological finds show the *Durotriges* may have resisted the Second Legion at Maiden Castle near modern Dorchester. If this was the case – and what was believed to have been Maiden Castle's 'war cemetery' may have only been a civilian burial place – the defenders were probably defeated by the Second Legion's superior weaponry, discipline and training. Later, around AD 70, the *Durotriges* were again defeated at South Cadbury just over the present Somerset border. Probably they had revolted.

However, there is no evidence of conflict in *Dumnonia* apart from a very unreliable medieval tradition. Possibly there are undiscovered battle sites; perhaps the *Dumnonii* saw resistance was futile and wisely came to terms. It is also possible that they co-operated with the Second Legion against the *Durotriges*, or had made a treaty with the Romans even before the invasion of AD 43, as the *Atrebates* of parts of what is now Surrey and Berkshire had done.

Certainly, the Romans established forts in *Dumnonia*, the most important of which was at the existing Dumnonian settlement of *Isca* (Exeter). The fort overlooked Exeter Quay, enclosing 1.5 ha. Finds of Hellenistic coins show that *Isca* was well established as a port with overseas trade. Possibly the small fort predated the full scale legionary fortress, which enclosed 15 ha and was built around AD 50.

It is uncertain how the Roman army established itself at Exeter, but it is clear why it did so. There is no evidence of Dumnonian resistance, but the map clearly shows the Second Legion not only gained a base from which to dominate the south-west peninsula, but a first class defensive location on a hill and protected by the river Exe (which was much wider then than now) to the west. Combined with their port just downriver at Topsham, they could readily ship supplies into Exeter and land troops. They could also intimidate the British and fall back to their fortress if necessary.

By around AD 120-30 *Britannia* was much pacified and Rome had influenced – or perhaps seduced – several generations of Britons. Exeter, its role as a frontier fortress largely obsolete, was now radically redeveloped. The future city was enlarged to 38 ha as the capital of the *civitas* (cultural and economic unit) of *Dumnonia*, to include a basilica, town hall, forum and that great symbol of civilised life, a bath house. Previously surrounded by an earth bank, Exeter gained a substantial stone wall around AD 200. Although this defence has been upgraded and repaired many times, large elements of Roman masonry remain.

Communications were vital to the Roman Empire. Everywhere they went, Roman armies built roads. The Fosse Way, the great cross-country Roman road from Lincoln, terminated at the naval base of *Moridunum* near Axmouth. It was greatly superior to existing British cross-country tracks. A westward branch of the Fosse Way led on to Exeter. Remains of it were discovered at Axminster when the modern bypass was built,.

Altogether, nine roads radiated out across Devon from Exeter, linking it with the rest of *Britannia*. One road led into Cornwall via the fort at North Tawton. Another road led to Bath and the Midlands and one to Topsham. There was a road to Dorchester, and a south-western road led over Haldon to Teignbridge. The foundations of a Roman bridge have been discovered at Kingsteignton.

Many Romano-British sites in Devon were occupied long after and often long before the Roman invasion and there is much continuity between the Iron Age and the Saxon period. Whilst Roman remains proclaim a technologically superior and literate urban civilisation, the whole Roman period, or 'Roman Interlude' as leading British archaeologist Barry Cunliffe called it, is best understood as part of Britain's historical evolution rather than as an abrupt and total change.

A good example is the site of the Roman villa complex at Seaton. It had been successively occupied from the late Neolithic. Just before the Roman conquest, there was an Iron Age farming settlement here, whose circular houses were of timber with thatched roofs. They were used long into the Roman period, but were replaced about AD 150-250 by at least three ranges of long stone buildings. These included a bath house with a hypocaust heating system. At least one room had a fine mosaic. A tile of the Augustan Second Legion (the one led by Vespasian) was also discovered. A cottage was built on the site in the medieval period, followed by a housing estate in the late 20th century.

Romanised life did not suddenly vanish when the Empire abandoned Britain in the early 5th century, but it was probably already in decline and then faded out in the coming centuries. The period between the withdrawal and the Anglo-Saxon subjugation of Devon in the 7th century may fairly be called a Dark Age because of the paucity of written sources and archaeological evidence.

Devon and Cornwall were at least partly Christian before St Augustine was sent by the Pope to convert the heathen Anglo Saxons in 596. Surviving Celtic church dedications testify to the evangelising work of Irish, Breton and Welsh missionaries during the Dark Ages. There are over forty Celtic church dedications in Devon, such as St Budeaux in Plymouth – originally 'St Budoc's hide' and Landkey near Barnstaple, meaning 'St Ke's church'.

However, as a source of historical evidence, church dedications are flimsy. Old dedications have sometimes been forgotten or changed. For example, St Winwaloe's at Portlemouth was long called St Onolaus's – though the original attribution has been reinstated recently. Several Devon churches are dedicated to St Petrock, but his cult continued until the 16th century Reformation. In short, a Celtic foundation cannot be blithely assumed for every church with a Celtic dedication.

3 Anglo-Saxon Devon

Fortunately there is more written material between the 7th century and the Norman Conquest of 1066. The *Anglo-Saxon Chronicle* is the richest source, especially for Anglo-Saxon conflicts with the British and Vikings. However, written evidence is still sparse compared with later centuries. Historians continue to debate the nature of the Saxon 'conquest' or 'occupation' of Devon and the survival or otherwise of the native British and their culture.

Conflict appears to have been spread over a century and more. In 568, the *Dumnonii* manned Exeter's city walls against Cealwin, King of Wessex and again in 632 against Penda, King of Mercia. King Cenwealh of Wessex defeated the *Dumnonii* at Pinhoe in 658 and again at Crediton in 661. Cenwealh was probably the founder of Exeter Abbey, c670-90. Shortly after, St Boniface (a native of Crediton) was educated there under Abbot Wolfhard.

'Centwine drove the Britons as far as the sea' according to the *Anglo-Saxon Chronicle* entry for 682. In 710, 'Ine and Nunna his kinsman fought against Geraint, King of the Britons'. According to another source (Florence of Worcester) Geraint was killed in this campaign, which probably brought remaining areas of Devon under the authority of Wessex. However, the Dumnonians won a victory in 722 at *Hehil*, an unidentified location.

British resistance continued and evoked a reprisal in 815 when King Egbert of Wessex raided in Cornwall 'from east to west'. In 825 the Cornish raided into Devon but were defeated at Galford near Lewtrenchard. Thirteen years later Egbert defeated them at Hingston Down just west of the Tamar. It was only in the reign of Athelstan in the 10th century that Cornwall was finally subdued, with the Tamar fixed (with a few small exceptions) as the county boundary.

Whether these widely spaced conflicts between Wessex and Dumnonia amounted to a full-blown conquest of Devon (let alone of Cornwall) is debatable. Battles feature largely in the *Chronicle*, but it is possible that much peaceful penetration of Devon by Saxon settlers happened unrecorded, and not unlikely that the majority of the population remained largely unchanged but merely adopted the newly dominant language.

Most Devon settlement names are Old English, a strong indication of Saxon linguistic and cultural dominance, especially when compared with Cornish place names, which are mainly British and strikingly different. Although some Devon names may have been coined for wholly new settlements, many must have replaced existing British names. British names form but a tiny fraction of Devon's village, hamlet and farm names – though many more British names survive for natural features such as rivers. Some scholars contend this place name evidence shows the Saxons drove the Dumnonians wholesale out of Devon into Cornwall and Brittany, or even slaughtered large numbers. Other authorities argue the contrary, that the survival of British names in remoter parts of Devon – Trusham and Dunchideock in the Haldon hills, Charles and Landkey in North Devon, for example – proves communities of Dumnonians lived on (though probably with inferior status) over most of the county.

Meanwhile, Devon emerged as an entity, distinct from Cornwall and from other English counties. From 851 the *Anglo-Saxon Chronicle* refers to 'the men of Defenascire'. With a few minor aberrations (some not corrected until 1966), the present boundaries of Devon were drawn in Saxon times, as were those of other English counties.

Devon was brought under the authority of the Catholic (as distinct from the Celtic) church in 705 when the new see of Sherborne was created to govern the whole South West. In 909 Sherborne was split into smaller bishoprics, including the new see of Crediton. In 1050 Bishop Leofric merged St Germans (in Cornwall) and Crediton, moving his see to Exeter. This bishopric covered all Devon and Cornwall until the see of Truro was created in 1876.

Except for the crypt at Sidbury and a few fragments in Exeter, nothing of the many Saxon church buildings remains in Devon. Probably all Devon's nucleated villages had a church by 1066, but many were built of wood or cob and were replaced by more durable stone churches after the Norman Conquest. Devon also had a number of important minster (monastic) churches, not only at Exminster and Axminster, but at Crediton, Braunton, Plympton and Coryton.

Whether predominantly Saxon or British in character, Devon was certainly not Viking. Although a high percentage of place names in northern England, East Anglia and the East Midlands are Danish or Norwegian, reflecting widespread Scandinavian settlement there, Devon has very few Norse names. These are almost entirely confined to the coast. Lundy, for instance, is Old Norse for 'Puffin Island'.

The Vikings did not settle in Devon, but they often raided and in doing so helped to forge an emerging 'English' identity. First recorded in the *Chronicle* raiding the Isle of Sheppey in 835, Vikings attacked Devon in 851, but were defeated by men of Devon under ealdorman Ceorl, at *Wicganbeorg*, probably near Paignton. Exeter's turn came in 876, when Vikings attacked the city and overwintered there, but were ejected by King Alfred the following summer.

In 878, Odun, Earl of Devon, and his thanes defeated the Viking host at a spot between Appledore and Northam known as 'Bloody Corner', now marked by a roadside plaque. The Danish leader, Hubba, was killed, but some Danes escaped in their longships. Although the Danes again attacked in 893, targeting Exeter and a fort on the north coast, nearly a century of peace followed.

The next Danish offensive came in 981, when 'much destruction was done everywhere along the coast, both in Devon and in Cornwall', according to the *Anglo-Saxon Chronicle*. Danes sailed up the Tamar in 997 'burning and slaying everything that they met.' Repulsed at Lydford, a fortified English settlement where a memorial stands near the church, the raiders sailed off with great plunder, including that of Tavistock Abbey, which they had burnt to the ground.

In 1001, Vikings sacked Teignton (Kingsteignton) and besieged Exeter. Failing to breach the city walls, they pillaged the villages around. Men of

Okehampton Castle, the largest in Devon, began as a motte-and-bailey castle with a stone keep and was developed into a luxurious residence by Hugh Courtenay, Earl of Devon, in the 14th century

Devon and Somerset fought them at Pinhoe, but were defeated. Pinhoe was burnt. In revenge England's King, Ethelred the Unready (which meant ill-advised) ordered the massacre of the many Danish settlers in his realm in 1002, including the Danish King Svein's sister. He further provoked King Svein by marrying Emma of Normandy (a rival power) and giving Exeter as a wedding gift to his new Norman bride. Svein attacked Exeter, an attractive target with its mint, and laid siege. Emma's Norman bailiff, Hugh, treacherously enabled the enemy to break into the city. The siege had already cost many lives, but Svein ordered Exeter's survivors to be massacred, its houses burnt and its churches pulled down.

Reconciliation came when Canute succeeded his father, Svein, and married the widowed Emma. He became king of England in 1016, atoned for Svein's atrocity in Exeter and rebuilt the abbey church. In 1019, Canute became King of Norway and Denmark too. This is not surprising as half England was former Danelaw and deeply influenced by Viking settlement. Indeed, the whole country looked set to become a permanent part of the Scandinavian world until England was conquered by William Duke of Normandy.

4 Medieval Devon

After William's famous victory near Hastings in 1066, English resistance continued, not least in Devon. Exeter was the centre of the Western Rebellion, 1068-69. The citizens held the city in great force, strengthening the walls and towers and encouraging other towns to defy the Normans. As the largest town in Devon, Exeter had to be subdued.

Hastening back from Normandy, King William demanded an oath of fealty from Exeter's chief citizens. They refused. William advanced with an Anglo-Norman force and laid siege for eighteen days before Exeter surrendered on favourably negotiated terms. The Normans immediately began building Rougemont Castle on the highest ground within Exeter's walls. Not one to dilly dally, William moved west to subdue the rest of Devon and Cornwall, ordering castles at Totnes, Launceston, Barnstaple and Okehampton to overawe the natives.

Within two generations of the Conquest, the Normans had built at least twenty castles around Devon. Most were erected quickly with earthen ramparts forming a tall motte, with a wooden keep on top, and a ditched bailey defended by a wooden palisade. Some were later replaced by stronger stone fortifications and more castles were added. Substantial castle ruins can be visited at Barnstaple, Tiverton, Berry Pomeroy, Hemyock, Plympton, Exeter, Totnes, Okehampton and Lydford.

Some castles remain as earthworks. Holwell castle at Parracombe in North Devon has its motte ditch partly cut through rock, making it particularly deep and strong. As well as building new castles, Norman lords updated some existing forts, especially Iron Age ones. Blackdown Rings near Loddiswell is one example (see page 8).

Medieval Devon was dominated by great feudal lords from their imposing castles and fortified manor houses such as Compton, Bickleigh and Dartington – all well worth visiting. At the top of the hierarchy were (and still are) the Courtenays, Earls of Devon. They owned estates all over Devon and castles at Tiverton, Okehampton, Powderham and Plympton, giving them both wealth and a strong military grasp.

Other powerful Devon families, whose influence lasted for centuries and in some cases to the present day, included the Mohuns, Dinhams and Fortescues. Among Devon knights there were Fulfords, Kellys, Edgecombes, Aclands and Fursdons, who all took their names from their estates. Many of these old Devon surnames survive. Most are also place names. The Fursdons of Fursdon near Thorverton, for instance, trace their unbroken ancestry to Walter de Fursdon, 1259.

Overall, Devon has the largest concentration of post-Conquest place names in England. The most noticeable are Norman-French feudal names joined to earlier Saxon or British place names and proclaiming ownership. At Bovey Tracey and Nymet Tracey, the manors were held by the de Tracy family. Similarly, the Ferrers owned Bere Ferrers and Churston Ferrers and the Courtenays Sampford Courtenay.

William I's formidable survey of his new kingdom, *Domesday Book* (1086), shows that the great majority of Devon estates had passed to Norman owners. Although this probably left the harsh conditions of daily life unaltered for people at the bottom of the social pyramid (the great majority), such a massive forced transfer of land was only rivalled by Henry VIII's Dissolution of the Monasteries.

The Church was a great power. Medieval bishops of Exeter were magnates, owning over 40,000 ha in Devon and Cornwall. Only the Courtenays

15

A print showing Tavistock about 1830. The Abbey was a Saxon foundation, and the town grew up to serve it

had greater estates in Devon than the Bishop of Exeter. The monastic houses (Tavistock, Buckfast, Glastonbury and Horton) held nearly 17,000 ha between them. All told, the church holding in Devon was nearly one sixth of the recorded total for the county.

Domesday Book also shows that Devon as a whole was taxed at a low rate for its size; it was underdeveloped and poor compared with the richer Midland and Eastern counties. Wealth from land was unevenly distributed. Plough teams, an indicator of fertile ground and thus wealth, were naturally concentrated in the most productive areas, especially the Vale of Exeter and between the Teign and Dart, along with some of the best North Devon lowlands. Sheep were mainly kept in arable districts, where land use was rotated. *Domesday* indicates there was more arable farming in medieval Devon than today, probably because most food was both produced and eaten locally. However, West Devon, the Culm Measures and the Dartmoor borders were cattle country even in those days. Many estates there had no plough teams.

Devon was one of England's most thinly populated counties in 1086, with approximately 70,000 inhabitants (compared with 1.1 million in 2000). Vast areas, perhaps half the county, were uncultivated. Devon's population increased greatly between 1086 and the Black Death, the devastating plague of 1348-49. Large areas were brought into cultivation and thousands of new farms created in what W G Hoskins called 'a colonisation movement'. For example, the hamlet of Dunnabridge high on Dartmoor did not exist in 1304 and was described as 'new' in 1306.

This newly cultivated land was typically divided into the small fields separated by high hedgebanks that still characterise most of Devon. Medieval open fields, which remained the norm in large areas of southern and midland England until the great enclosures of the 18th and 19th centuries, were enclosed in Devon from the 13th century. Communal agriculture was replaced by individual farming. Braunton Great Field is the

The new boroughs were self-governing and appointed officials such as the Ale-taster – an institution still celebrated at Ashburton today, with appropriate seriousness

exception – a rare surviving medieval strip field. Parts of the Great Field's 126 ha are divided into 86 strips, marked by low, unploughed boundary banks called 'landscores'. Walking over it is a journey into the past.

Although most of Devon's large villages and hamlets already existed by *Domesday*, Devon had only five towns. The biggest, Exeter, had a meagre population of around 1500; the defensive *burhs* created by King Alfred, Barnstaple, Totnes and Lydford, each had only a few hundred people and newly created Okehampton fewer still.

A remarkable 61 new boroughs were created in Devon between 1086 and 1348. Several, South Zeal, Bow, Newton Poppleford and Honiton for instance, can be recognised by their characteristic settlement patterns. Most of the old houses face directly onto one long main street. They are built on 'burgage plots' – strips of land the width of the house but as much as a furlong (200 m) deep. The houses doubled as shops and workshops for a range of traders and artisans.

Many Devon 'towns' failed to develop beyond villages, but wherever self-governing borough status was combined with a suitable position and economic opportunity new towns were successful, Dartmouth and Plymouth outstandingly so. They, with Exeter and Barnstaple, developed

Originally built of wood, Bideford Bridge was rebuilt in stone around 1280 and has been repaired and widened many times since. Its early construction testifies to the commercial importance of the town

overseas trade, exporting Devon cloth and tin and importing wine from Aquitaine.

Devon's expanding maritime trade was inseparable from its increasingly important naval role. Medieval England relied heavily on armed merchant seamen and their ships, licensed as 'privateers', for defence. Dartmouth's much respected leading merchant and privateer John Hawley (c 1342-1408) embodied this duality. He was fourteen times Mayor of Dartmouth and twice MP.

Dartmouth with its superb anchorage rapidly emerged as a leading port. In 1147 an international force of 164 ships assembled there and sailed for the Second Crusade. Thirty-seven ships left the Dart to join the Third Crusade in 1190. Dartmouth played an important, often leading role, in England's wars from then on, not least in the Hundred Years War, when it sent 31 vessels to the Great Blockade of Calais in 1346.

Most Devon towns and villages played a part in the growing cloth trade, a domestic industry with international exports. The invention of water-driven tucking (fulling) mills in the 13th century brought about a rapid dispersal of cloth making to suitable sites by Devon's many fast-flowing rivers. Exeter, with a concentration of mills on Exe Island, became one of England's leading cloth towns and remained so until the 18th century.

The earliest reference to Devon's tin industry is in the Pipe Rolls of 1156. Production boomed for 50 years, before it was overtaken by Cornish tin. Because tin output fluctuated greatly, it was often a supplementary job for Dartmoor farmers and labourers, though some hardy men earned a generally meagre existence solely from tinning. Tinners were renowned for their independence and enjoyed a variety of astonishing privileges, confirmed by royal charter in 1201 as 'ancient custom'. Exempt from proceedings in any court of law but their own Stannary courts except in cases of life, limb and freehold, tinners were also exempt from ordinary taxation and from all tolls in towns, fairs and markets.

Stannary law was administered from Lydford Castle. Built around 1200 as both courtroom and prison, it was also the administrative centre of the Royal Forest of Dartmoor. Like Exmoor Forest, this was a privileged hunting preserve on the wildest moorland, guarded against poaching by draconian penalties. Lydford Castle had a grim reputation. Richard Strode, MP, found out about Lydford Law first hand in 1508 when he was imprisoned by the tinners for criticising the way the debris from their work clogged local rivers. Eventually, he got free and was instrumental in passing the law giving MPs the right to freedom from civil action while Parliament is sitting.

The first Warden of the Stannaries was appointed in 1198. Wardens continued to regulate tin mining until the 19th century. Sir Walter Raleigh was the most distinguished man to hold the post, which was considerably more than a costume drama. Until 1838, the law required all tin to be assayed and sold through Devon's Stannary towns – Chagford, Ashburton, Tavistock and Plympton. Inevitably, some tin was smuggled out of England without duty being paid.

The Black Death of 1348-49 was a social and economic catastrophe. Around half Devon's population died. Some settlements, many new and on marginal land, were abandoned, over 130 on Dartmoor alone, Houndtor hamlet being a prime example. Farms were left without tenants. The tin trade came to a standstill.

Devon's population began to recover over the next two generations and with it agriculture and the tin and cloth trades. The building boom of the 15th century is one measure of recovery. Construction of secular and especially church buildings stimulated the whole economy and left Devon with a lasting heritage of late Gothic architecture. Nine Devon churches out of ten were affected by the great wave of rebuilding that swept on until the Dissolution of the Monasteries in 1536-40. Here is material proof of the power both of the church and of popular religious feeling, which does much to explain the religious conflicts of Tudor and Stuart Devon.

5 Tudor Devon

Devon was not immune either from political conflict. In 1497, twelve years after Henry VII's victory at Bosworth had supposedly ended the Wars of the Roses, Perkin Warbeck, a pretender to the throne, brought fighting to Devon. Warbeck attacked Exeter with 4-5000 men. Repulsed, he retreated to Taunton and surrendered. Henry VII marched the prisoners back to Exeter. He had the leaders hung, drawn and quartered, but the lesser rebels were pardoned.

Devon was much more directly concerned in the Prayer Book Rebellion of 1549. The rebellion was a popular revolt against the imposition of radical Protestant reforms centred on the new Prayer Book. Since it threatened the fragile authority of the boy king Edward VI, and the Reformation in England, it was brutally suppressed.

Henry VIII's break with Rome in 1536 and his declaration of himself as Head of the Church of England had launched the Reformation in England, beginning with the Dissolution of the Monasteries. In Devon, monastic lands were valued at £6700p.a. in 1536, a huge sum, five times the land revenues of Devon's richest family, the Courtenays. Henry sold most of the land, mainly to his supporters. The wealthy and ultra-Protestant Russell family were the greatest single beneficiaries in Devon. Lord John Russell later led the royal army that crushed the Prayer Book Rebellion.

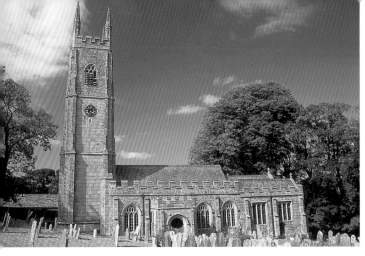

It was here at Sampford Courtenay that the Prayer Book Rebellion began in 1549, and where the final defeat of the rebels occurred a few weeks later.

Tableaux in the church graphically depict the events

In 1547 chantries were suppressed in Devon as elsewhere. Next, images were removed from parish churches. The new Prayer Book was one step too far for some of Devon's innately conservative and religious people. In Sampford Courtenay it was first used on Whit Sunday 1549. Outraged parishioners compelled the Rector to return to the Latin book the next day, complaining that the service was 'but a Christmas game'. Magistrates came to Sampford to enforce conformity. Tempers were lost and a local gentleman was killed on the steps of Church House.

Farmers, labourers and workmen, led by a few gentry and priests carrying banners and swinging censers, marched on Exeter. At Crediton, they joined three thousand Cornishmen, incensed at the imposition of a Prayer Book in English, a foreign language to many. While the rebels fruitlessly besieged Exeter for five weeks, Russell mustered a royal army, consisting mainly of foreign mercenaries. Far better equipped and trained, they beat the rebels in three battles in East Devon. Exeter was relieved. The courageous rebels were finally defeated at Sampford Courtenay. Russell hunted down the remainder. Naturally, their demands were never met. They had died calling for all the old ceremonies to be restored, with the Mass in Latin, the reserved Sacrament over the high altar, images once more, and all English scriptures to be withdrawn. They also asked for the restoration of Plympton and Tavistock monasteries.

The events of 1549 certainly did not end religious division in Devon, but over the next century the county underwent a sea change in beliefs. Large parts of it emerged as Puritan and Parliamentarian strongholds, but the picture was far from simple, as the next chapter will show.

Despite civil and religious strife, Devon prospered. During the 16th century it emerged as a leading county. In terms of naval defence and contribution to England's emerging role in overseas discovery and colonisation, it was second to none. Devon's population now rivalled Yorkshire's

In Exeter (left), Dartmouth (right) and Totnes, 16th and early 17th century prosperity left a wonderful heritage of buildings

and possibly Kent's. This growth was achieved despite plague, which made periodic returns until the later 17th century. These could be as locally devastating as the first Black Death.

The county's tin trade boomed in the early 16th century. Although tin production later slumped, the cloth trade rose and more than compensated for it. In 1500 Devon woollens made up 10% of English cloth exports, whereas the 1380 figure had been a meagre 1%. Devon's domestic cloth trade was probably three times as great as its export market. This industrial and commercial growth led towns like Totnes and Exeter, Devon's wealthiest cloth centres, to expand, leaving a wonderful legacy of Tudor and Stuart buildings.

Prosperity also came from farming. More Devon acres were brought under cultivation, many new farmhouses built and medieval ones improved with such novelties as chimneys, second storeys and entrance porches. Many still stand, sometimes with prominent datestones.

The 16th century was a great period of maritime expansion, especially for Devon, which contributed largely to the booming Newfoundland cod fishery. By the 1570s, fifty English ships were making the dangerous but lucrative seasonal voyages to Newfoundland. Often, they traded dried cod in Mediterranean ports on the homeward voyage and picked up a secondary cargo of wine or fruit.

The county's social and political connection with Newfoundland is particularly strong. It was claimed as England's first colony by a Devonian, Sir Humphrey Gilbert, in 1583. Some Devonians settled there. Many Newfoundlanders can still trace their Devon ancestry.

Elizabethan Devon was second only to London in merchant shipping tonnage. Its shipbuilding industry was fuelled by growing demand for ships. With the Spanish threat increasing, Plymouth overtook Dartmouth as Devon's premier naval port. Although vulnerable to south-westerly gales, Plymouth offered easier access and a much larger anchorage. As the home port of many fishermen it could readily supply sailors for war, and leaders too. Francis Drake and John Hawkins, who became Treasurer of the Navy in 1578 and Comptroller in 1589, were Plymouthians.

The nineteenth of July 1588 was Plymouth's finest hour. More than sixty ships assembled in the Hamoaze and Cattewater to repulse the Spanish Armada, the largest war fleet ever seen. King Philip II's grand design was to sail up the Channel and link with the Duke of Parma's troops in the Spanish Netherlands, invade England, dethrone Elizabeth and force the country back to Catholicism.

Victory over the Armada preserved England's identity and opened the gates to a new destiny, a seaborne empire to eclipse all others. Queen Elizabeth knighted Sir John Hawkins for his services in defeating the Spanish, whilst Francis Drake, already knighted for his epic circumnavigation of the globe, became legendary for his courage and *sang froid*. Many dismiss the tradition that Drake insisted on finishing his game of bowls on Plymouth Hoe before weighing anchor. However, Drake was well aware that strong south-westerly winds had bottled up the English fleet and the only way to get the ships out of Plymouth Sound would be on a powerful ebb tide. On 19 July high tide was at 10.31pm. When the Armada was sighted and Drake informed, it would thus have been either dead low water or a rising tide.

Born around 1541, Drake already had vast sailing experience – unlike the Armada's commander, the Duke of Medina Sidonia. He first achieved fame with his West Indian voyages of 1570-72 and earned Spain's hatred by harassing her shipping. He took over where another Devon seaman, Captain John Oxenham, had left off. Oxenham was the first Englishman to sail the Pacific, but his 1574 expedition to Darien ended with his capture and execution by the Spaniards.

Setting sail from Plymouth in 1577, Drake was altogether more successful. From the Straits of Magellan, he plundered his way northwards as far as what is now British Columbia. By the time he reached Drake's Bay (San Francisco) he had lost all of his five ships except the *Golden Hind*, but had a stupendous haul of looted treasure. The safest way home was the boldest – to sail westwards around the world. Drake dropped anchor in Plymouth Sound in 1580 and received a hero's welcome. He became Mayor of Plymouth and an MP. With his fortune in Spanish treasure, he bought Buckland Abbey from Sir Richard Grenville.

Drake was also instrumental in having 'Drake's leat' authorised by Parliament and built in 1590-91, but he manipulated the project for his own profit and for the benefit of his water-mills. Pocketing half the money Plymouth had raised, Drake failed to provide either the naval victualling yard at Lambhay or the built-up areas of the city with water as originally planned. Some of the excess water was offered to the public after it had driven Drake's mills – but only 30 homes had been connected by 1600.

Sir Richard Grenville built Bideford's fortunes through overseas voyaging and plundering Spanish colonies. Proposing an American colony, Grenville commanded the fleet of seven ships taking his cousin Walter Raleigh's abortive colony to Roanoke, Virginia, in 1585. Bringing home a number of prizes, Grenville surprised Bideford by christening a native American 'Raleigh'. He died in 1591 on his ship fighting impossible odds against fifteen Spanish vessels and was later celebrated by Tennyson's poem, 'The *Revenge*'.

Grenville was indeed a man of fanatical courage, as the poem proposes, but also of 'intolerable pride and insatiable ambition' as a contemporary described him. It is probable that he disobeyed the orders of Admiral Lord Howard who, appreciating the overwhelming superiority of the Spanish force, had ordered a tactical withdrawal from Flores in the Azores. Although the other English ships escaped, the *Revenge* fought on till she was a dismasted wreck. Whilst the Spaniards offered an honourable surrender, Sir Richard was all for sinking his ship. He was prevented by his officers and given the best possible care by his foes, who recorded his last words, full of pride in his achievement and scorn for the men who after fighting heroically had chosen not to die – but the scorn was omitted from the English translation and from Tennyson's poem.

Another North Devon seaman who combined trade with plunder was Richard Dodderidge. In 1591 Dodderidge brought home the 70 ton *Spirita Sancta* of Lisbon as a prize. She was laden with gold and civet and carried 72 cwt (3.5 tonnes) of 'elephant's tooths', as well as 183 cwt (9 tonnes) of cochineal – both typical imports from Guinea. The West African coast became the prime source of slaves for the New World, though a few came to Europe as servants. Indeed, Black Africans were baptised in Barnstaple in 1596, 1598 and 1605.

Stephen Burrough of Northam explored the Arctic seas to reach Russia and (somewhat unimaginatively) named the most northerly cape 'North Cape' in 1553. Burrough was appointed Chief Pilot of England. His brother William attempted to find a route to Cathay. William later became Comptroller of the Queen's Navy and was Vice Admiral under Drake on the famous attack on Cadiz in 1587, the 'singeing of the King of Spain's beard'.

Born by the Dart, John Davis was the most celebrated navigator of his day. His quest to find the 'North-West Passage' – a supposed short cut between Canada and the North Pole to China – led him to discover the Davis Strait between Greenland and Baffin Island. His charts, books and notes were of immense value to other navigators then and later.

The last and most brilliant of Devon's famous Elizabethans was Sir Walter Raleigh: soldier, sailor, navigator, poet, historian and courtier. Born in East Budleigh in 1554, he achieved fame as a soldier in France and Ireland. Raleigh was appointed Captain of the Guard and found great favour at court – but lost it and was jailed for marrying Bess Throckmorton, one of the jealous Queen's maids of honour. Rehabilitated, he led the sack of Cadiz in 1596, but was imprisoned by James I on trumped-up charges in 1603. Released in 1616 for a last and futile attempt to find El Dorado in Guiana, he was beheaded on his return.

Taken as a group, Devon's seamen undeniably had faults. Drake, Grenville and Dodderidge were pirates; Hawkins was the first of many Englishmen to trade in African slaves and so proud of it that he had an African in chains on his crest; Raleigh massacred his prisoners at Smerwick on his Irish campaign. Notwithstanding, their achievements were huge and inseparable from the Elizabethan age, in which England emerged from the insular medieval world to begin a new destiny as an international sea power.

Raleigh's birthplace, Hayes Barton in East Budleigh parish

The defining period of the 17th century was the Civil War, 1642-46, here commemorated at Bovey Tracey

6 Stuart Devon

Although civil wars and religious divisions dominated the politics of Stuart England, Devon's industry and trade continued to prosper in the early Stuart years, and again late in the 17th century. However, during the middle decades the disruption and destruction wrought by the Civil Wars proved a severe setback, economically as well as socially. The county was deeply divided in matters of religion and politics and many battles large and small were fought on Devon soil.

England's political situation deteriorated badly during the 1630s. King Charles I's attempt to rule without Parliament caused widespread discontent, not least in Devon. His imposition of Ship Money – ostensibly a tax to finance the navy – without sanction of Parliament, was especially resented. Religion was a second bone of contention. Puritanism had risen as a powerful force in Devon and there was widespread dismay at the High Church tendencies of the King and his appointee as Archbishop, William Laud. William Strode and John Pym were among the most outspoken and determined critics of Charles and Archbishop Laud. Both were staunch Puritans and Devon MPs. Strode represented Bere Alston, Pym Tavistock. They were among the five MPs Charles tried to arrest in 1642.

Strode had been arrested in 1629, protesting angrily against arbitrary taxation and innovations in religion. He spent the next eleven years in jail. On his release, he campaigned for the execution of the King's favourite, Strafford, and urged preparations for war. Later, he showed great zeal in the prosecution of Laud, who was also executed. Pym led the Parliamentary opposition to Charles in the crucial years leading to war in 1642. He too initiated legal attacks on Strafford and Laud, as well as organising the loans and taxes which financed Parliament's armies.

Pym and Strode always knew where they stood, but loyalty to King or Parliament was a fraught and complex matter for many Devonians. The issue has been analysed in detail by historian Mark Stoyle (see Bibliography). With families as well as communities often divided, generalisations falter. On the whole, Devon was more Parliamentarian than Royalist. Religion was the most likely indicator of allegiance – religion and politics being inextricably entangled in 17th century England.

Powerful families led Parliament's cause in Devon: the Russells (Earls of Bedford), Rolles, Bampfyldes, Drakes, Martyns, Strodes and Northcotes. Tenants naturally followed their landlords; it was difficult to do otherwise. But there were great Royalist landlords too: Aclands, Seymours, Carys, Fulfords, Heles, Pollards and Poles. Among the middle classes, those involved in industry and commerce usually sided with Parliament.

Although Devon suffered less than some counties, the war took a heavy toll in blood, money and material destruction. Throughout the struggle, Devon parishes were burdened with supplying men, financing troops and providing living quarters for soldiers. Not surprisingly, many Devonians sympathised with the Clubmen – political neutrals who called a plague on both houses. Eventually, the Clubmen favoured Parliament, because the New Model Army under Fairfax and Cromwell was better disciplined and less likely to pillage than the Royalists, whose 'General in the West', Sir Richard 'Skellum' Grenville, thoroughly deserved his evil reputation.

With its marches and counter marches, its sieges and reliefs, its skirmishes and confused engagements, the Civil War in Devon often had an intensely local flavour and is difficult to summarise. However, the successful defence of Plymouth for Parliament was clearly crucial. Although long besieged, it was well entrenched and valiantly defended, and constantly re-supplied by sea. Holding the most important naval base in the West, Parliament never entirely lost Devon, despite early Royalist victories.

The battle of Sourton Down on the north-western edge of Dartmoor in April 1643 was inconclusive, but the Royalist victory in May at Stratton (just over the Cornish border) opened Devon to their advance. Nearly the whole county fell to the Royalists. Bideford, Barnstaple, Appledore, Dartmouth and Exeter all surrendered. By the end of 1643 the entire South West was in Royalist hands – except the ports of Plymouth, Lyme and Poole. In summer 1644, Parliament took the offensive. The Earl of Essex swept successfully through Devon, but he over-reached himself invading Cornwall and suffered humiliating defeat at Lostwithiel.

After notable victories in the North and Midlands at Marston Moor and Naseby, Parliament's New Model Army was free to march west in the summer of 1645. Bristol, Bath, Bridgwater and Taunton fell to them. They hit Devon in October, taking Tiverton on 19 October. On 24 October, General

Fairfax was joined by Oliver Cromwell as his second-in-command. Exeter was besieged and finally retaken in April 1646, along with Barnstaple.

Meanwhile, the retreating Royalists suffered defeat at Bovey Heathfield. Dartmouth was recaptured in January 1646. Hopton's defeat at Torrington gave the *coup de grâce* to the Royalist cause in Devon, but the speed of the Royalist collapse reflects both the superiority of the New Model Army and general war weariness in Devon, exacerbated by Royalist exactions and robbery. With the surrender of Fort Charles, Salcombe on 7 May 1646, the war in Devon was over.

In addition to those killed and injured, the war left Devon with many destroyed and damaged buildings. Plymouth and Exeter had suffered much destruction. Axminster was burnt down. The church at Torrington had blown up with 200 prisoners inside. Communities and individuals had large debts. Exeter merchants Roger Mallock and Robert Walker were among prominent Royalist supporters heavily fined as 'delinquents' – £1600 and £900 respectively.

The Commonwealth (1646-60) inherited not only a long history of political and financial mismanagement from Charles I's rule, but also the impoverishment and discontent which invariably follows protracted warfare. Moreover, the fighting did not cease in 1646. Further campaigns were fought in Scotland, Ireland and at sea, imposing more heavy burdens. Fortunately, there was no more fighting on Devon soil, but garrisons remained in several towns, including Exeter and Plymouth, giving the county an air of military occupation – never popular with civilians.

The landing of William of Orange, 1688, a print from a painting by Turner

Royalist supporters were generally ousted from power, especially in the Church. About one third of the Devon High Church clergy (including the poet Robert Herrick of Dean Prior) were ejected and replaced with Puritans. After the Restoration, the boot was on the other foot. Herrick and many other High Churchmen were reinstated and 132 recalcitrant Puritan clergy were forced to resign by the Act of Uniformity.

Cromwell died in 1658. His son Richard failed to inspire confidence. General George Monck of Merton in Devon, aided by his relations William Morice from Werrington and Sir John Grenville of Stowe near Kilkhampton, largely engineered the Restoration of Charles Stuart. As King, Charles rewarded all three.

Dissenters did not fare so well, losing the brief and rather imperfect toleration they had enjoyed during the Commonwealth. Until King William III's Toleration Act in 1688, they ran the risk of harassment, imprisonment or transportation for practising their faith.

Loughwood Baptist Meeting House near Dalwood still testifies to these difficult times. One of England's earliest non-conformist meeting houses, Loughwood (first recorded in 1653) was hidden away in formerly wooded country close to the county borders. The congregation could flee to either Devon or Dorset, depending on which county their tormentors came from. Now owned by the National Trust, the meeting house is open to the public.

Charles II, a secret Catholic, was succeeded by his openly Catholic brother James II in 1685. The Duke of Monmouth, eldest of Charles' thirteen illegitimate children, had already toured the West triumphantly. Posing as the Protestant champion, he chose to land at Lyme in 1685 and seek local support in his attempt to take his uncle's crown.

Many Devonians, notably from East Devon cloth towns such as Colyton, followed Monmouth to defeat at Sedgemoor. The names of 730 of these Devonians are known; eighteen were wounded at Sedgemoor, nine killed elsewhere. Following Judge Jeffreys' infamous 'Bloody Assizes', 56 Devonians were executed. Some were dismembered and their quarters hung up in prominent locations around the county as a hideous warning to others. Seven died in prison, 148 were transported and 40 lost all their lands. Whilst others were flogged or fined, 72 were pardoned – his Honour was open to bribery. Many rebels went on the run until a general pardon was proclaimed in 1686.

Confident that he too would find support in the West, William of Orange landed near Brixham on 5 November, 1688 (the anniversary of the failed Catholic plot to blow up Parliament in 1605). William, another nephew of King James, succeeded where his cousin Monmouth had failed in seizing the crown and thus he has a statue in his honour in Brixham harbour.

Devon ports which thrived on overseas trade still retain some splendid 17th century buildings.

Topsham (above right) was virtually rebuilt between 1660 and 1730. The town had particularly strong trading links with the Netherlands through Devon's prosperous cloth industry, which accounted for a sixth of England's woollen market.

Many Topsham buildings, notably the so-called 'Dutch houses' on the Strand, contain Dutch bricks, brought home in ballast.

Exeter's Custom House (middle photo) dates from 1681.

Dartmouth's 'Butterwalk' (below right) is actually four merchants' houses from the 1630s

From Brixham, William advanced cautiously to Newton Abbot and then Exeter under the banner GOD AND THE PROTESTANT RELIGION. After some understandable hesitation (the memories of Judge Jeffreys being fresh) people of all conditions showed their support. They included the ambitious John Churchill (later Duke of Marlborough) who had fought against Monmouth.

Under King William III war and religion continued hand in hand, but the action took place outside England. Recent battles with the Dutch were tacitly forgotten and Charles II's secret Treaty of Dover with France was null. Instead, England and the Netherlands waged war on Louis XIV. In Ireland, William's forces defeated a smaller Catholic army led by the man he had deposed, King James II. This Battle of the Boyne on 12 July 1690 (an anniversary still both celebrated and execrated in Ulster) marked a critical stage in England's subjugation of Ireland.

Meanwhile, the new English political and religious settlement or 'Glorious Revolution' as it was dubbed by its Whig supporters, granted toleration to all Protestants. Devon was now better able to concentrate on its developing industry and trade, especially with King William's native and ardently Protestant land, the Netherlands.

Devon ports which thrived on overseas trade still retain some splendid 17th century buildings. The 'Dutch' houses in Topsham and Exeter's Customs House (1681) are testimony to wealth and trade, as are the merchants' houses in Dartmouth, notably the Butterwalk. Equally impressive are Bideford's Bridgeland Street (begun 1697) and the Horwood and Penrose almshouses in Barnstaple, whilst Appledore's Beaver Inn recalls the valuable North American furs brought home in locally built and manned ships. Sugar and in particular tobacco were the principal imports from the American and Caribbean colonies, with Bideford's trade in tobacco exceeded only by London's. Devon exported woollens and trade goods to the colonies and cloth to Europe.

The rich Newfoundland fishery was a mainstay of Devon's maritime economy down to the 18th century, stimulating seamanship, shipping and trade. Devon ports, led by Topsham, Teignmouth, Dartmouth and Bideford dominated it. By 1700, 200 Devon ships were regularly engaged. The biggest from Bideford was 220 tons and carried 65 crewmen and 20 guns.

Devon exerted a strong influence all along the North American Atlantic seaboard, as evidenced by many familiar place names, including Plymouth and Barnstable in Massachusetts and Torrington, Connecticut. New Hampshire has Appledore Island, Plymouth and Exeter. New York State also has a Plymouth, as do North Carolina, Vermont and Pennsylvania – which has Devon too. Biddeford is in Maine. North of the border are Dartmouth, Nova Scotia and Torbay, Newfoundland.

7 Georgian Devon

Between 1689 and 1815, Britain was at war with France for 67 out of the 127 years, in seven separate wars. These wars raised Devon's strategic importance greatly. Torquay emerged as a naval station and Dartmouth built ships for the Navy, but the greatest developments were at Plymouth.

Dock (called Devonport after 1824 and part of Plymouth from 1914) sprang up as a modern naval yard. In 1733 its population was 3000, rising to 12,000 in 1780 and 24,000 during the Napoleonic Wars.

Devonport/Plymouth played a crucial role as Britain's leading western port, repairing, supplying and building warships and stationing men. Ships sailed from Plymouth Sound to fight all over the world, guard the Western Approaches, blockade France and deter invasion.

Devon's merchant marine was also strategically and economically vital. Possibly one Devon man in every five made his living from the sea directly or indirectly. In 1788 Devon ports had 707 registered ships, employing 4500 men. Small vessels, in which a great deal of trade and inshore fishing was done, were not usually registered. Many more people were employed building ships, loading and unloading them, and in associated trades such as rope making, sail making and ships' supplies.

Smuggling was a huge but (by its very nature) unquantifiable trade. It was at its height during the 18th and early 19th centuries, when the exorbitant cost of war led the government to impose swingeing duties on a host of goods – an incredible 1425 items by 1815. The opportunities for smugglers were immense. Perhaps a quarter of Britain's import/export trade was illegal. For some commodities, tea in particular, the figure may have been two thirds. Huge quantities of spirits and tobacco were also smuggled and offered to eager buyers at a fraction of their taxed price. With its host of skilled mariners and secluded landing places, Devon profited greatly. Smuggling was probably the county's leading 18th century industry.

Smuggling was pervasive, with a network of shippers, financiers and distributors at all levels of society. A parliamentary committee reported 300 English vessels involved full time in smuggling – in effect, a second merchant navy. French brandy was Devon's market leader. Excisemen estimated in 1783 that half England's smuggled brandy came via Devon and Cornwall; eighteen million litres annually, or six bottles for every English adult.

Smuggling operated against a background of widespread poverty. It offered adventure and luxuries such as brandy and tobacco normally reserved for the rich, but also far more money than Devon sailors, fishermen or farm labourers could normally earn.

Devon's population nearly doubled during the 18th century, but living standards generally declined and food shortages recurred. When

The original Axminster carpet factory was built by Thomas Whitty in 1755. An account in 1780 says the carpets were made 'by the pliant fingers of little children'. The building we now see was rebuilt after a fire in 1827

war disrupted imports, grain prices soared. Bread riots were endemic. Thomas Campion of Ilsington was hanged in 1795 for his part in the riot at Bellamarsh Mill, Bovey Tracey. Typically, the rioters demanded a 'fair' price for bread and saw the millers and merchants as villains hoarding grain and forcing up prices.

Some Devon industries prospered and some declined during the 18th century. On the debit side, Devon's cloth production declined as England's industrial centre of gravity shifted north, closer to the coalfields which fuelled an increasingly mechanised industry.

Although Dartmouth engineer Thomas Newcomen was a pioneer in steam engineering and his 1712 reciprocating engine revolutionised deep mining, Devon's own hard rock mining production fell. By contrast, Devon's ball clay and china clay industries grew dramatically. Although clay had been dug around Petrockstow from medieval times, the massive reserves of the Bovey Basin were first worked extensively from 1730. Teignmouth had a considerable export trade in clay by 1750. Three potteries were established in Bovey Tracey between 1760 and 1800.

Carpet making flourished in Axminster, where Thomas Whitty set up the first carpet factory in 1755. Although production failed in 1835, it was revived after 1945 and 'Axminster' is again a household name.

Hand-made lace, possibly introduced to East Devon in Elizabeth's reign by Flemish refugees, developed in the 17th and 18th centuries. Demand fell in the early 19th century, affected by new and much cheaper machine-made lace. Leicestershire lace maker, John Heathcoat took over one of Tiverton's last woollen mills in 1816. His factory remains the town's major industry – though production is now focussed on modern textiles.

Although much Devon cider was consumed locally, often as part of farm labourers' wages – a fuddling four pints daily was common down to the early 20th century – large volumes were also exported as far as London

32

'The York Hotel and Library, Sidmouth' as they were in 1830. Construction of the York, Sidmouth's first hotel, began in 1807 at the height of the Napoleonic wars

and Newfoundland. Most was made in the South Hams, Taw Valley and East Devon. Production reached 45 million litres in 1750, equivalent to 150 litres for each of Devon's 300,000 inhabitants.

Oddly, war also started Devon's tourist trade, which became increasingly important in Victoria's reign and Devon's largest industry in the 20th century. War and subsequent naval blockades made Continental travel difficult, often impossible. Wealthy English travellers followed George III's example, patronising English seaside resorts and sea bathing.

Exmouth, Teignmouth and Dawlish grew in the late 18th and early 19th centuries, when their modern history and Devon's tourist trade began. 'Some persons of condition' were observed visiting Exmouth in 1750. New streets of elegant houses were later built to accommodate them, The Beacon, Louisa Terrace and Bicton Place.

In Dawlish, Dawlish Water was straightened in 1803 so that it ran through The Lawn, previously a marsh. The Strand and Brunswick Place were laid out on either side and a new seaside town for genteel visitors was created. Old Dawlish was left clustering around St Gregory's.

The 1803 *Guide to Watering Places* declared: 'The prosperity of Teignmouth in great measure depends upon its summer visitors,' whilst the *Gentleman's Magazine* of 1792 stated: 'Its houses, to what they were, are palaces, its inns are good and its accommodation equal if not superior to any summer resort in Devon.'

In 1752 the *Gentleman's Magazine* had observed that 'a Londoner would no more think of travelling to the West of England for pleasure than he would of going to Nubia.' Considerable road improvements made by turnpike trusts, together with a growing Romantic taste for the picturesque, probably did more than anything to induce London gentlemen to patronise Devon.

Devon has the highest road mileage of any county except Yorkshire, but

Exeter's quay area, now hugely popular with locals and tourists alike, is dominated by two five-storey warehouses built in 1835 – but notice the Georgian terrace on the hill above, ideal town houses for merchants

before the late 18th century, even the main roads were appalling. Seasoned traveller Celia Fiennes commented in 1698: 'Went to Plymouth 24 long miles, and here the roads contract and the lanes are so exceeding narrow… the ways became so difficult… just a track for one horse's feet.' Despite increased wealth and population, most Devon roads were little better than in medieval times. Bulk transport was usually by packhorse; individuals rode or walked. Wheeled vehicles were rare, almost unheard of in remoter areas – a severe loss to the local economy as a horse can typically pull five times the load in a cart that it can carry on its back.

From the 17th century some Devon towns had a weekly carrying service to London. The first passenger coach service from Exeter to London started in 1658. It took four days. By 1764 this was reduced to two days, in 1784 to 32 hours. In 1828 the *Devonport Mail* achieved 19 1/2 hours.

Exeter, like Plymouth, was connected to most principal British towns by coach, with 60 daily services, eight of them going to London, but a bone-shaking London trip on the *Telegraph* cost 70 shillings inside and 35 shillings outside – the latter being around a month's wages for a labourer.

Devon's first turnpike trusts, Exeter, Honiton and Axminster, were set up in 1753, collecting tolls from travellers to improve access to the towns. By 1815 most of Devon's towns were connected to 776 miles of turnpikes. The trusts had gravelled existing roads and trimmed the hedges, but little more. Nearly 6000 miles of Devon roads had not been turnpiked and there were many more miles of tracks. This was not a road network and was not designed as one.

The George Hotel in Axminster, a typical coaching inn, large and functional – the extension on the right contains the town's Assembly Rooms in which local society could meet, dance, and promote marriage alliances

Road building entered another phase after the Napoleonic Wars. Many completely new roads were made, especially along river valleys, to avoid the narrow courses and steep gradients of what were often very ancient tracks over hills and ridges. Some of these roads remain among Devon's busiest routes. The Copplestone to Barnstaple route, which superseded the old road over the hills between Morchard Bishop and Chulmleigh in 1831, is a good example.

As well as 1142 miles of roads, Devon's 32 turnpike trusts built 400 toll-houses. Some 80 survive. Scattered around the county, they can often be recognised by their angled sides. Several retain their signboards, showing tolls. New roads also demanded new bridges. Many of Devon's road bridges date from the turnpike era, including Cowley (1814), Shaldon (1827) and Totnes (1828). Models of civil engineering and elegance, they still carry main road traffic.

8 Victorian Devon

Coaching reached its zenith in the 1830s. Travel was faster and more comfortable than ever before. This was the era described by Charles Dickens in *Pickwick Papers*, in which the Eatanswill elections and the Fat Boy were inspired by his Exeter journeys. Exeter was one of England's leading coaching centres, liberally provided with coaching inns. Many survive in the city and all along Devon's old coaching routes. Often, they can be identified by their high arched coach entrances, former courtyards and stables, or by names such as the Coach and Horses or the Post Boy, the London Inn or the Plymouth (after destinations).

For most of inland Devon, roads provided the only transport. The county had just two horse-drawn railways, successful but of only local importance.

The Beam Aqueduct on the Rolle Canal, built in 1823. Its route was subsequently used for the Bideford-Torrington railway

The Haytor Tramway of 1820 linked to the canal at Teigngrace. It carried Dartmoor granite, as did the Plymouth to Princetown Railway (1826).

Although canals were an integral part of the Industrial Revolution in the North and Midlands, they never competed seriously with roads in Devon. However, Devon did have the first English cut to carry bulk transport – the Exeter Ship Canal (1566). The canals from Tavistock to Morwellham on the Tamar and from Teigngrace to the Teign provided cheap transport for minerals and stone.

All three canals joined navigable rivers, as did the Rolle Canal, which ran for six miles from the limekilns at RHS Rosemoor near Great Torrington to Landcross, where it joined the River Torridge. Completed in 1827, it carried lime, coal and clay until closed in 1871 to make way for the Bideford to Torrington railway. The less successful Grand Western Canal, originally planned to cut across the south-west peninsula, was eventually limited to an isolated 17 km stretch from Tiverton to the Somerset border. The railway rendered it obsolete, apart from very local traffic.

Steam trains revolutionised Devon's transport. The mainline railway from Bristol reached Exeter in 1844. The chief engineer was I K Brunel, whose controlling and inspiring influence is apparent all along the south Devon line, not only in its engineering, especially the beautiful and innovative coastal line via Dawlish and Teignmouth, but also in its station architecture. Brunel's magnificent Tamar Bridge (1859), which enabled the line to continue into Cornwall, still carries mainline traffic and bears his name on its remarkable iron arch. However, Brunel's bold experiment with atmospheric traction proved impracticable and only operated from September 1847 to June 1848 between Exeter and Newton Abbot.

Thereafter, expansion was piecemeal, with several railway companies involved. Crediton gained the railway in 1851, Barnstaple in 1854. In 1860 the line from Exeter via Honiton and Axminster linked Devon to the shorter southern route to London. The Okehampton and Tavistock railway to Plymouth was not completed until 1890 and the Teign Valley line until 1903. Devon's maximum railway mileage was only reached in 1925.

Far faster and cheaper than road transport, trains were also more comfortable. Standard journey times from Exeter to London were soon reduced to a mere five hours, including stops, making them the fastest in the world, a quarter the time of comparable coach journeys.

Rail had a strong, often a profound impact on every place it reached. Wherever roads ran parallel to railways, turnpike income fell markedly. The Cullompton Trust and the Plymouth and Exeter Road Trust were among the hardest hit. Devon's last turnpike trust was wound up in 1889, its duties assumed by the increasingly powerful Devon County Council.

Tourism could never have developed as it did without railways. Cheap rail travel opened Devon's coasts to ordinary people for the first time, making places such as Exmouth, Dawlish and Teignmouth popular family destinations. Railways and associated tourism fuelled the expansion of Devon's coastal towns. Devon resorts and industrial centres connected to the rail network, such as Newton Abbot, witnessed a population explosion. Torquay, joined early to the railway in 1848, grew by a staggering 1750% during the 19th century. Exmouth (rail connection 1861) took second place. It grew by 806% and Teignmouth by 380%.

North Devon's resorts gained the railway later and their development lagged behind. Murray's *Handbook to Devon* of 1895 complains 'the railway from Barnstaple has given increased facility for reaching [Ilfracombe]; and

Bridestowe Station, west of Dartmoor, on the LSWR main line from Okehampton to Plymouth

Dartmoor's 19th century industries included the age-old grazing of the moor, but attempts were made to industrialise the extractive industries.

Top left: Granite quarried at Hay Tor was transported by horse-drawn tramway to Teigngrace, then sent by canal to Teignmouth Docks

Middle left: Opencast tin mining. These buddles (circular pits in which the ore was separated from the waste material) were in fact installed in the early 20th century at Hooten Wheals mine on Dartmoor, which was later known as Hexworthy Mine

Bottom left: Dartmoor Prison at Princetown. The cheap labour was used in an attempt to bring the moorland to agricultural productivity – with little success

those who desire quiet and comparative solitude will do better to pitch their tents at Westward Ho or at Lynton.' Ilfracombe had a railway link in 1874, Lynton in 1898 and Westward Ho! in 1901. So much for Murray.

As readers of Murray's *Handbook* were well aware, Devon was an increasingly popular destination. More people could afford a holiday and more had holiday leave to enjoy, though paid leave was rare till the 1920s. Devon had 1000 hotels and lodging houses in 1856, but this had risen to 3000 in 1914.

Devon's population nearly doubled in the 19th century from 340,000 to 660,000. This is even more remarkable as 371,000 Devonians emigrated. This emigration was chiefly from Devon's villages. It was partly caused by rapid population increase, partly by decline of some traditional industries.

Devon's cloth industry, for centuries the county's economic mainstay, dwindled. Agriculture entered a long depression from the 1870s, when cheap New World imports undercut Devon products, especially grains. From a peak figure of 272,000ha in 1872, Devon's arable farmland entered a decline not reversed until the 20th century's world wars demanded it – and then only temporarily. In 1889 the area of Devon under grass exceeded the arable area for the first time.

Half of Devon's emigrants went to London, some only as far as neighbouring counties. Others found a new life in the New World. Many Devon villages have fewer inhabitants today than in the 1851 census, especially in remote parts of the county. There are many variations from one village to another but Thorverton, a big agricultural parish in the fertile Exe Valley, can serve as an example of the great changes in 19th century rural Devon.

In 1801 Thorverton had 1168 inhabitants, rising to 1511 in 1851. In 1901 the figure had fallen to only 813, falling further to 674 in 1961 as mechanisation reduced the need for agricultural labour. However, inward migration, especially by the retired and by commuters, had helped the population to rise to 916 by 2000.

Like most Devon villages, Thorverton was a self-contained community. *White's Directory* of 1851 shows it had four bakers, three blacksmiths (one was a part time dentist – no doubt he had a gentle hand), three butchers, four grocers, two saddlers, two shoemakers, four tailors, two wheelwrights and two plumbers. Thorverton had its own parson, curate, surgeon, solicitor, accountant, builder, nurseryman, agricultural machine maker, maltster and druggist. It had three inns and three schools. Happily it retains the three pubs and its primary school: many Devon villages have lost school, pub and shop.

Whilst Devon villages declined, Exeter's population grew from around 20,000 in 1800 to 59,000 in 1901, reflecting Devon's increasing urbanisation. However, Exeter had already been overtaken by Plymouth. Between

1815 and 1914 the population of the three towns (Plymouth, Devonport and Stonehouse) rose from 56,000 to 209,000. Plymouth was one of Victorian England's most densely populated cities.

As Plymouth had an alarmingly high mortality rate – closely associated with overcrowding – much of its growth was achieved through immigration. Thousands of immigrants came from famine-stricken Ireland – only Liverpool among British ports had a bigger Irish population. Many others came from Cornwall and West Devon, especially whenever mining suffered one of its many setbacks.

Devon's 19th century mining industry presents a mixed picture as new finds were made, old seams were exhausted and prices fluctuated – sometimes wildly. In all, there were between 200 and 300 mines at work in the county at various dates, employing up to 6000 men, besides women and many more workers in related industries.

Whilst Dartmoor tin prospered and then declined, production of some other minerals, including manganese, silver, arsenic and fluorspar, fared better. Tamar Valley copper mining was the greatest success by far, certainly for shareholders, though the miners were badly paid and strikes commonplace. Devon Great Consols alone produced 750,000 tons of high grade copper ore. For a time, it was the largest copper mine in the world, with Devon and Cornwall producing more than half the globe's copper between them.

Devon Great Consols employed up to 1100 men and the original £1 shares reached £800 six months after opening in 1844. Unfortunately, mining is a boom and bust business. The mine's production fell and it closed in 1901. (It reopened between 1915 and 1930, but little production was achieved.) Tavistock settled back as a market town. Its superb Victorian square remains a souvenir of the copper bonanza. A copper statue of the immensely wealthy Duke of Bedford has pride of place. Bedford was a member of the Russell family who had been granted the copper-bearing lands of Tavistock Abbey at the Dissolution of the Monasteries.

Many Devon miners emigrated like their Cornish cousins. Some struck lucky, mining in South Africa, Australia or North America. In the 20th century, imported metals increasingly undercut those of Devon's remaining mines. When the haematite mine near Hennock closed in the late 1960s, hard rock mining in Devon appeared finished. Bramble-strewn mine ruins remain all over the county, especially on Dartmoor.

9 Devon since 1900

The whole of Britain has changed greatly since Victoria's reign. The character of that change in Devon is unusual, although closely paralleled in Cornwall. It is inseparable from the county's favoured geographical position and its magnetic attraction for tourists, retired people and (in recent years particularly) seekers after the good life.

In 1901 Devon's population was 622,196, rising to 823,800 in 1960, a 32% increase. It increased a further 39%, to 1,143,000 by 2010, one of the fastest rates of growth for any English county. Inward migration is the chief cause, giving parts of Devon an increasingly urban character. The population has become markedly older than the national average.

Until the later 20th century, this population influx was dominated by retired people. The M5/A38 corridor has been a constant population attraction, especially on its southern side. In some south coast resorts such as Sidmouth and Seaton, an astonishing 50% of the population is retired. From 1971, deaths in Devon exceeded births.

However, in the late 20th century, the focus of population increase changed from Devon's big towns and popular coasts, spreading to more remote and rural areas. The overall trend of rural depopulation in the South-West was reversed in Devon in the 1970s and '80s. Recent population maps suggest that rural areas have the fastest population growth. As plans to build new towns at Sherford near Plymouth and Cranbrook near Bradninch are carried through, Devon's population will grow faster than ever.

Most migrants first see Devon as tourists. Over seven million visitors come to Devon yearly – more than six times the county's population. During the 20th century, tourism became increasingly important to Devon's economy, as rising real incomes made it possible for more people to take more holidays and paid holidays became usual. In 1925 1.5 million British workers enjoyed paid vacations, rising to 11 million in 1939.

Tourism changed in several ways. During the 19th century railways had made cheap travel and thus seaside holidays possible for more people. Naturally, they were particularly drawn to resorts served by the railways such as Teignmouth, Torquay and Dawlish. These resorts remained popular in the 20th century but, with increased car ownership, tourists visited and stayed in more varied locations. Most visitors stayed in hotels and boarding houses in the 19th and early 20th century. However, self catering accommodation, including caravans, camp sites and chalets, became increasingly popular with car-borne tourists.

From the 1970s, cheap air travel to foreign resorts, especially in Spain, created the air-borne tourist and gave Devon's seaside resorts tough competition. However, the county remains popular with visitors. Many come

The LSWR service from Exeter to Chagford was introduced on 1 June 1904, so this photograph may well have been taken on that day. The railway companies developed local bus services to enable more people to access the railways

to Devon for second holidays, often outside the traditional summer holiday months, especially if they own second homes in the county. Although Devon's seaside is still the greatest draw, the county's rich heritage and beautiful landscape are also major attractions. Inland Devon, particularly Dartmoor, has drawn increasing numbers of visitors, as have historic homes and gardens, as well as theme parks, museums and visitor centres.

The growth in Devon's population and its tourist industry are inextricably bound to the massive increase in road transport and the modernisation of the county's road network throughout the 20th and into the 21st century. Whether this can be sustained as oil supplies begin to diminish, leading to increased fuel prices, remains to be seen.

Although railways did not reach their maximum mileage in Devon until 1925, competition from road transport had already started in earnest. A number of rural motor bus services were operating before 1914. The Great Western Railway built 420 new halts and platforms between 1903 and 1947 to respond to local transport needs, including links with buses – and introduced its own bus services from 1903.

Devon's railways became part of the nationalised network, British Railways, in 1948. Unhappily, the lack of investment suffered during wartime continued. Several branch lines closed during the 1950s, including the Princetown Railway, the Teign Valley and Dart Valley lines and the Moretonhampstead branch. In 1963 British Railways' new Director, Dr

Richard Beeching, drove through massive railway closures. Devon lost further lines, including those in the Exe, Avon and Culm valleys. There was also a rash of station closures, including main line stations between Totnes and Plymouth. Train services suffered. Passenger and goods traffic fell.

Had but a fraction of the investment which has been poured into roads by successive governments gone to railways, Devon's network might have survived intact. The successful re-opening of the Dart Valley and Paignton to Kingswear railways as tourist attractions with steam locomotives suggests the potential of Devon's branch lines.

Motor cars first appeared in Devon in 1897, but their cost ensured they did not have such an immediate and dramatic impact as railways. Only the rich could afford cars until mass production slashed relative costs in the 1920s. Even so, car ownership did not become the norm until long after 1945.

Devon's 13,100 km (8200 miles) of roads were incredibly quiet by today's standards, even though all classified roads were surfaced with tarmac by 1939. Cars remained a novelty for many years. Exeter, for example, boasted twelve cars in 1904, rising to 225 in 1912 and 1300 in 1920. By 1947, the figure was 4000, rising steeply to 15,000 in 1960 and 40,000 in 2001.

Despite lower than average incomes, car ownership in Devon is above the national average. Between 1950 and 1979 the volume of Devon's motor traffic increased by 600% and the number of vehicles rose 450%, to 270,000. This rise has continued inexorably with rising real incomes and declining public transport especially in rural areas.

In 2001, Devon's 458,536 households owned 528,864 cars and vans – an increase of 113,948 vehicles in only ten years. Vehicle ownership, as with other trappings of wealth, was not evenly spread. A significant minority of households (23%) did not own a vehicle; 48% owned one, 24% two, and 6% of households owned three or more vehicles.

Road building has gone hand in glove with rising vehicle numbers, spurred on by the peculiar congestion problems of holiday traffic, which on a summer Saturday crowds the M5 with six times the usual winter volume of vehicles. The M5 itself was largely built to relieve summer logjams. It reached Exeter in 1976 and extended over the Exe in 1977. The A38 was made a dual carriageway to Plymouth in 1974 and later upgraded to the 'Devon Expressway'. In 1987 the 'North Devon Link Road' was built, followed by the highly controversial Okehampton Bypass in 1988 which sliced into the Dartmoor National Park.

Devon's road building reached its peak in the 1980s under the Thatcher regime, its philosophy expressed in the White Paper *Roads to Prosperity* (1989).

Only in the 1990s was there recognition that road building might worsen traffic congestion and that transport policy would need to be radically rethought for the 21st century. The growing awareness of the environmental damage wrought by road transport has added another dimension to the issue.

Agriculture, at the heart of a traditionally rural Devon, has had mixed fortunes over the past century. Expanded rapidly to keep the nation fed during the attempted German U-boat blockade of 1917-18, farming suffered a severe depression in the '20s and '30s. Modernised and expanded again for strategic reasons in the Second World War and for decades afterwards, agriculture changed almost out of recognition. Mechanisation led to a massive decline in the agricultural workforce and the merging of farms, with many farmhouses and labourers' cottages changing ownership, often being bought by incomers.

On one hand, this has helped preserve Devon's rich stock of historic buildings, including those in cob, thatch and local stone so characteristic of the county. Conversely, the historical continuity of many Devon farmsteads and villages – often stretching back to medieval or even earlier times – has been disrupted or destroyed.

Farming entered difficult and uncertain times at the turn of the century, when Devon's many beef and dairy herds were particularly hard hit by the epidemic of foot-and-mouth disease. Prices fluctuate, but at the time of writing an extended period of low prices offered to farmers by increasingly dominant supermarkets had depressed incomes and forced many Devon farmers to abandon their dairy herds. Rising world food and fuel prices complicate the picture, and their long-term effects are hard to predict.

Devon's fishing industry has also had very mixed fortunes. Brixham had 213 trawlers in 1910. The First World War was a disaster, with many trawlers sunk by U-boats and many fishermen called up for naval service. The Brixham fleet declined to only six boats in 1939, but was revived and modernised with diesel-driven boats after the disruption of the 1939-45 war.

Brixham, as it appeared in June 1965. Although one of Britain's most valuable fishing ports, it now faces an uncertain future along with the whole fishing industry

The Sherman tank at Slapton, a memorial to US servicemen who lost their lives there in the preparations for D-Day

The Devonport Dockyard, a bastion of Britain's naval defences, especially of the Western Approaches. But the Dockyard too cannot be sure what the future may hold

Brixham rose to be one of Britain's most valuable ports again. The port itself was expanded in 1971 and 1985 and the fleet consisted of 115 boats by 1997. However, declining fish stocks, combined with more stringent EU quotas and a dramatic rise in the cost of diesel fuel trouble all Devon's fishing ports at the time of writing (2011).

Devon was deeply affected by both world wars. Although loss of life, as testified by war memorials in every town and village, was greater in the First War, air raids brought war to the heart of Devon's towns – Exeter and Plymouth especially – in the Second.

Britain's chief western naval base, Plymouth, mourned the Battle of Jutland in 1916, when five Devonport-manned ships were lost. Devon's merchant marine and fishing fleet also suffered severely. A hundred fishing boats and a similar number of merchant ships were sunk by enemy action off Devon and Cornwall at the height of the U-boat blockade.

Devon's sailors and soldiers served with distinction in 1914-18. The Devonshire Regiment, first raised in 1685 to help crush the Monmouth Rebellion, added the *Croix de Guerre* to its seven battle honours gained in the Peninsular War (1809-14). This was the French government's recognition of the Devons' courage at Bois des Buttes in May 1918. Two Devonshire men were awarded the Victoria Cross. Private Veale saved a wounded officer during the Battle of the Somme in 1916, in which the Devons suffered heavy losses, and L. Cpl. Onions played a leading role in capturing German prisoners in 1918.

Whilst several Devon towns, notably Teignmouth and Dartmouth, were badly damaged by German bombing in the Second World War, the destruction wrought on Exeter and Plymouth was especially severe. Their rebuilding has aroused controversy, but none deny that Devon's two cities are much altered. Brash post-war shops in concrete and glass dominate the centres of both. Plymouth expanded enormously after 1945, with new housing estates to replace the densely packed streets that were lost.

For its size, Plymouth was the most heavily bombed city in England, a back-handed compliment to the vital part it played in Britain's naval defence. Between November 1940 and May 1941 the heart of old Plymouth was largely destroyed. During 59 bombing raids 1228 tons of bombs were dropped on the city, killing 1172 civilians, destroying 3700 houses and damaging 72,000 more. Plymouth servicemen could barely recognize their home city when they returned from overseas.

Exeter was targeted for its cultural rather than its very limited military importance in the 'Baedeker Raids', intended to demoralise Britain by destroying its most beautiful cities. The Luftwaffe raided Exeter seventeen times between August 1940 and December 1942. German airmen devastated 15ha of central Exeter with 75 tonnes of bombs, killing 156 people and injuring 500 more. Exeter lost 400 shops and 1500 houses, with another 2700 severely damaged.

Dartmouth played a key naval role in both world wars and saw the greatest volume of shipping it had ever known between 1939 and 1945. In 1942 Philips' shipyard was attacked by German aircraft and 23 people were killed. A year later 14 died when central Dartmouth was bombed.

Dartmouth was packed with ships and servicemen in the build-up to D-Day, when a great triangle of land from the coast by Slapton to Blackawton was requisitioned by the Allied forces. It consisted of seven parishes, 180 farms and some 3000 people and was chosen for its strategic position and resemblance to Normandy. A similar evacuation was carried out for training around Croyde, Putsborough and Woolacombe in North Devon.

Evacuation was especially traumatic for farmers, who had made a supreme effort to boost wartime food production. They now had to abandon their farms, lift their crops and find accommodation for themselves, their goods and their stock. People had just six weeks to pack up and leave in November/December 1943.

Tragically, some soldiers did not even make it to the grim battles in France. The Sherman tank at Torcross car park is a memorial to 946 men who died during Exercise Tiger in April 1944, when German E boats made a surprise attack on American landing craft off the Devon coast.

Devon was regimented to the needs of national defence. Plymouth dockyard alone employed 20,000 workers by 1945, but its workforce was progressively reduced as Britain's world military role shrank. Only 2000 workers were employed by 1999. However, despite deep defence budget cuts, revised plans and worries over an uncertain future, Plymouth and Dartmouth remain vital Royal Navy bases, with the Britannia Royal Naval College at Dartmouth the national centre for officer training. The Royal Marines have their permanent HQ at Lympstone and train on Lympstone Common, whilst Army training continues on Dartmoor. Devon also has a radar station at Hartland Point.

Devon's distinctive geography continues to shape its strategic role as it has in centuries past. Indeed, in reviewing Devon's long history, it is no exaggeration to state that geography and destiny have gone hand in hand. In attempting to describe what has made Devon unique among English counties I have been obliged to return again and again to the county's position in the south-west peninsula, in particular to the sea and Devon's two coastlines, with their natural anchorages and navigable rivers. If the history of an island nation has always been inseparable from salt water, the same is doubly true of its leading maritime county. There is every reason for believing this will continue to be so.

Select bibliography

Beacham, Peter (Editor), *Devon Building, an Introduction to Local Traditions*, Devon Books, Tiverton, 1990

Cherry, Bridget and Pevsner, Nikolaus, *Devon*, The Buildings of England series, reissued by Yale University Press 2004 (originally Penguin)

Duffy, Eamon, *The Voices of Morebath: Reformation and Rebellion in an English Village,* Yale University Press, 2001

Freeman, Ray, *Dartmouth and its Neighbours*, Phillimore, Chichester, 1990

Gill, Crispin, *Plymouth a New History*, Devon Books, Tiverton, 1993

Hoskins, WG, *Devon*, Phillimore, Chichester, 2003 (first edition David & Charles, Newton Abbot, 1954)

Hoskins, WG, *Two Thousand Years in Exeter*, Phillimore, Chichester, 1960, 1963 and 2004

Exeter's Princesshay development, new in 2007, includes shops with city-centre flats above. Its centrepiece is this view of the cathedral's Norman towers from Princesshay Square

Hoskins, WG, *Devon and its People*, David and Charles, Newton Abbot, 1959 and 1968

Ordnance Survey maps of Devon, first produced 1809. Reprinted and rescaled by Cassini (Timeline), 2005

Stanes, Robin, *A History of Devon*, Phillimore, Chichester, 1986 and 2000

Stoyle, Mark, *Loyalty and Locality*, University of Exeter Press, 1994

Sturt, John, *Revolt in the West: The Western Rebellion of 1549*, Devon Books, Tiverton, 1987